Rossella Panuzzo

Juanita
and her Alpaca

Discover my Peru

Terre des hommes
Protecting children together

▶ 2 Hello! My name's Juanita. I'm nine and I'm from Peru. I live in a small village called Chinchero, 30km from Cusco. My village is 3,762m above sea level, in the Sacred Valley of the Incas. In Chincero there's a fantastic market where you can buy authentic, local products.

Juanita

The Incas

Between the 13th and 15th century, the Incas were very important in South America. They lived in the Andes Mountains and spoke Quechua, a language which is still used today in Peru. The word 'Inca' means 'king' or 'emperor' in Quechua. In their cities the Incas built very big pyramids. The Spanish explorer, Francisco Pizarro, conquered the Inca Empire in 1532.

Cusco

Cusco was the capital of the Inca Empire. Its name means 'centre of the world' in Quechua. Today, Cusco is a wonderful city with a lot of interesting buildings to visit, like Qoricancha which in Quechua means 'Golden Courtyard'. In fact, in Inca times it was covered with  gold! It was once the most important temple in the Inca Empire. You can also see the Inca Rosa Palace, the Cusco Cathedral, and many other places.

The Salt Ponds of Maras

Maras is a town in the Sacred Valley of the Incas. Here you can see the very old salt ponds. There  are about 3000 ponds that are made of salt water. The water evaporates and pink salt crystals are formed. They are very important for the local people. ⏹

Machu Picchu

▶ 3

Machu Picchu is often called 'the Lost City of the Incas' because nobody knew about it until an English man found it in 1911. Today it is a UNESCO World Heritage Site and one of the seven wonders of the world.

Life in the Andes

The Andes Mountains are very high so there isn't much air and the sun is very strong. However, the people and animals have learned to live with these problems.

Here are some of the most common Andean animals.

The alpaca

The alpaca is a typical Peruvian animal. It looks like a sheep but it's bigger and has a longer neck. Alpaca wool is soft and expensive. It is used to make coats, ponchos, sweaters, scarves and coats. Here you can see the colourful alpaca wool.

The llama

The llama is much bigger than the alpaca and its head is less rounded. It can weigh between 130 and 155kg and it can carry up to 96kg! Llamas are intelligent and friendly and can move very fast everywhere.

The vicuña

This animal is similar to the camel and it lives high in the Andes. During the Inca Empire, the Incas caught vicuñas to get wool from them. Vicuña wool was expensive at that time, and only the Inca king could wear it. ▪

▶ **4** Pedro is my older brother. My dad says that Pedro should start to work as a farmer in the *cancha* (a small piece of land), and keep sheep, llamas and alpacas, but he's only 12 years old. In this photo you can see Pedro and our little sister, Rosario. They are wearing typical Peruvian clothes.

Last night I couldn't sleep well. My alpaca was about to have her babies and I was really excited. Baby alpacas are called *cria*. They are so soft and fluffy! 'I hope she has two *crias*, so there will be one for Pedro and one for me', I thought. ◉

▶ 5 My dad is a farmer. He works in the fields and he grows potatoes, maize, beans and quinoa (a healthy grain). My aunt and my grandma take care of the sheep every day.

We get many things from our sheep: milk, meat and wool. We use the wool to make clothes and the typical coloured blankets called 'frazadas'. ◉

6 My grandma is very good at making 'frazadas' and sometimes I go with her to sell them at the market. In this photo you can see the loom that she uses to make the 'frazadas'. My sister, Monica, helps her. You can see Monica in this photo!

At home I share my bed with Monica. The bed is made of rope, wood and a lot of 'frazadas'. It doesn't have a mattress, but it's warm and quite comfortable.

▶ **7** This is a photo from last year. I'm with my friends. I'm the one who isn't wearing a hat. In our free time we make bracelets and necklaces with alpaca wool. Sometimes we make gifts for the alpacas.

After school, we do our homework and then we play together. Sometimes we babysit our little sisters. We play lots of games, but above all, they love playing on the swing! ∎

8 This is my house and you can see my mum. The houses in my village have a fireplace, which is nice, especially when it gets cold at night.

The houses are built of clay bricks that are made of mud and straw. These bricks are dried out in the sun. Each family builds its own house. Here, my dad is making bricks. ⬛

▶ 9

This is my classroom. We go to school from March to December. School starts at 7.30 a.m. and finishes at 1.30 p.m. so we study for 30 hours per week. We study Quechua and Spanish. In my classroom the children are different ages but we only have one teacher.

I get up really early in the morning to go to school. It takes about one hour to walk to school. When I see the rivers I'm afraid because I think of a story about two children, an old lady and a vicuña. Pedro told me this story! ▣

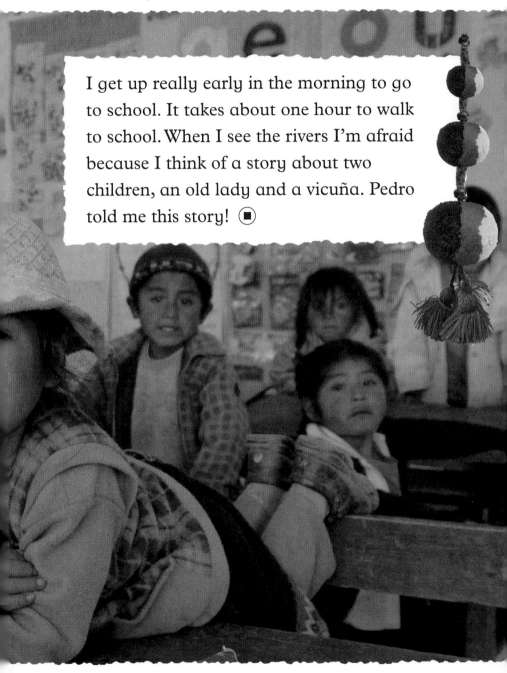

▶ 10 Once upon a time, two children – a brother and a sister – decided to leave their village. They were walking in the street, hand in hand, trying to be brave, when they met an old lady. She told them to go back home, because they could get lost. But the children didn't want to go back, so the old lady said:

'Along the way you will find three rivers: one is red, one is yellow and the other one has crystal clear water. Be careful! You must drink only from the last river, if not, terrible things will happen!'

11 The old lady was right. A little later, they arrived
at the red river and the boy was thirsty, but the
girl didn't let him drink from that river. Later,
they arrived at the yellow river.

The girl walked on, but the boy stopped. He was very thirsty, so he decided to drink a little water from the yellow river, forgetting the old lady's words. Then the girl stopped. She was worried because she couldn't find her brother. ◉

12 Far away, there was only a little vicuña running to the mountain. The girl was very sad and she started to cry. The little vicuña came near her.

The girl looked at it and she thought she knew its face: yes, it was her brother! She didn't know what to do, so she waited and then decided to go back to the yellow river. When she drank the water, she became a vicuña, like her brother, and they went together to the *Puna*, a faraway land in the mountains. ◉

13 And that's why they say that vicuñas look human: their eyes are black, like human eyes, and their neck is very soft. And when they cry, they're very sad. ◉

▶ 14 But I wasn't sad that night. I was excited! I was
thinking about my alpaca and I wanted to be
with her while she was having her *crias*. Mum
said that alpacas usually only have one *cria*, but
I hoped for two little twin alpacas!

The moon was big and full that night. Finally, I
fell asleep. Tomorrow I'll have a little alpaca!

The next morning I woke up very early and I ran outside. I couldn't believe my eyes... there were two little alpacas! They were small, with big black eyes and fluffy white wool... and I was so excited and happy! One for me and one for Pedro!

Maybe, when I grow up, I'll have a little vicuña too... like the one in the story! ■

Activity Pages

1 **Answer the questions.**

1 What country is Juanita from?

2 Where did the Incas live?

3 What does 'Inca' mean?

4 What did the Incas build?

5 What was the capital of the Inca Empire?

6 What is the name of 'the Lost City of the Incas'?

2 **Circle the correct word.**

Juanita's grandma is very good **1** *at / to* making 'frazadas'. Sometimes Juanita goes with **2** *his / her* grandma to sell them at the market. **3** *Your / Her* sister, Monica, helps to make the 'frazadas'. **4** *At / In* home, Juanita shares her bed with Monica. The bed **5** *doesn't has / doesn't have* a mattress, but it's warm and comfortable.

3 Complete the sentences and do the crossword.

1 This animal is similar to the camel.
2 It is a typical Peruvian animal and it looks like a sheep.
3 It is a UNESCO World Heritage Site.
4 Alpaca _ _ _ _ _ is expensive.
5 There isn't much _ _ _ in the Andes Mountains.
6 This animal is bigger than the alpaca.

4 Match the parts to make sentences.

1 ☐ Juanita couldn't sleep because...
2 ☐ Her alpaca was about to...
3 ☐ Baby alpacas are called...
4 ☐ Juanita hopes her alpaca...

a cria.
b has two babies.
c she was excited.
d have her babies.

5 **Match the objects to the descriptions.**

1 ☐ You sleep on this.   **a** coat
2 ☐ He/She works in the fields.   **b** bed
3 ☐ You can put this on your food.   **c** bricks
4 ☐ You wear this to keep you   **d** the
    warm.   moon
5 ☐ It's in the sky at night.   **e** farmer
6 ☐ You use these to make a house.   **f** salt

6 **Write a summary of the story about the vicuña.
Put the verbs in brackets in the past simple.**

One day two children **1** _____ (decide) to leave
their village. They **2** _____ (meet) an old lady.
The old lady **3** _____ (say): 'You will find three
rivers: one is red, one is yellow and one has crystal
clear water. You must only drink from the last river.'
Later, the boy and the girl **4** _____ (arrive) at
the red river. The boy **5** _____ (be) thirsty but he
_____ (not drink) the water. Later they
6 _____ (arrive) at the yellow river. The boy
7 _____ (stop) and **8** _____ (drink) some
water. The girl **9** _____ (cannot find) her brother.
She **10** _____ (see) a little vicuña. It **11** _____
(be) her brother. She **12** _____ (go) back to the
yellow river. When she **13** _____ (drink) the
water, she **14** _____ (become) a vicuña too.

COMPARING CULTURES

7 Machu Picchu in Peru is a famous World Heritage Site. Imagine you are planning a holiday to visit this important Inca city. Write a letter to Juanita asking her for information.

- Who / discover Machu Picchu?
- What clothes / items to bring?
- When / best time to visit?
- What / language people speak?

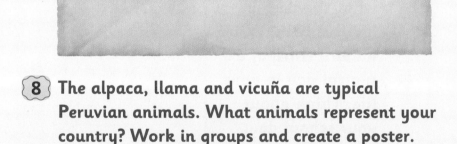

8 The alpaca, llama and vicuña are typical Peruvian animals. What animals represent your country? Work in groups and create a poster.

9 'Frazadas' are blankets made from sheep wool. Can you think of a typical product of your country/region? Share and compare your ideas with your classmates.

10 Juanita walks to school. It takes her about one hour. How long does it take you to go to school? How do you travel to school? Do a class survey and record your results on a bar graph.

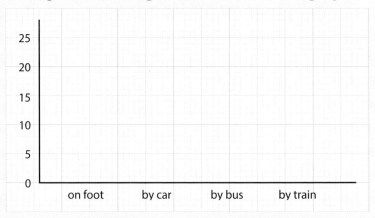

11 On pages 12-13 Juanita describes what she does in her free time. Write a diary entry of a typical day in your life. Think about your school day, lunch time, free time activities... How is it different or similar to Juanita's day.

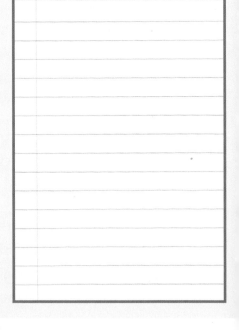